The Bliss Buddy Project

How Sharing Gratitude Increases Joy

Anne Sussman

ISBN: 978-172700024-5

Dedication

This book is dedicated to my Bliss Buddy, Jana Schey, my true friend, and to all the original Miami Bombshells for giving me wings and especially to Tammi Leader Fuller and the Campowerment Crew for pushing me out of the tree so I could fly.

Introduction

Does the world really need another book about gratitude? When I searched "gratitude" on Amazon.com, it yielded more than 13,000 books, so maybe not.

However, I believe this little book is different. Why? Because, by now, almost everyone knows that shifting into an "Attitude of Gratitude" offers many benefits. Research shows that grateful people tend to be happier, less stressed and kinder to others.

This is not a book about that research. If you're craving research, check out *Thanks! How Practicing Gratitude Can Make You Happier* by Robert Emmons.[1]

Have you noticed how some experiences are just more fun if you have someone to share them with? Telling someone about a moment of joy—even if you experience that delight all by yourself—makes you feel more connected, happier and more likely to savor it.

Sharing brings us great pleasure and helps us feel less isolated. Having a "Buddy" is the essence of this book. I hope the information here will be a light for you, a map to connect to the joy that is actually present in your life right now, if you only stop to notice it. I wish you peace.

The Gift of Meditation

We all have a small voice inside of us, one that comes from deep within our chest or belly, one that can sometimes start to get really loud. Some people call this intuition; others call it your authentic self. I believe that it's your soul. This is not the voice that talks constantly in your head all day. It's a voice that is heard only when you listen for it and are quiet enough to hear it.

I found my soul only after I committed to a daily practice of meditation and mindfulness. The chatter of my mind started to quiet and that small voice began to get louder and stronger, until its message became undeniable. First it said, "Quit your job and become a meditation teacher!" It was hard to listen. It seemed like a crazy idea. How could I leave my job running an office for an interior designer? I needed the money. To train to be a meditation teacher I'd have to go back to school. I hadn't been in school in 30 years, how could I go back to being a student?

So, I tried to ignore it, which worked for a little while. Yet every time I settled into meditation—that moment when I could be still and not listen to the incessant daily chatter in my head—the small voice rose up again, insistent.

Meditation had taught me that the thoughts in my head are not really *"me."* I knew that the small voice I was hearing was my essence, my authentic self, my SOUL.

I listened. I took the leap and became a certified meditation and mindfulness instructor. I have been happily and gratefully teaching ever since.

Lately, though, that voice has been calling to me again. "Write a book!"

Really? *Me?* Write a *book?* But as I have learned, when I listen, I become aligned with my purpose and that is how I found my new way to live—a way that brings me great joy. The idea of writing a book also terrified me. That fear made me absolutely sure it was what I should do.

I offer it to you, the reader, with sincerity and honesty.

Gratitude Is
the Foundation for Joy

I have found that sharing gratitude with another actually increases joy for both people. This practice keeps you accountable to another who wants to hear about your happiness—and share theirs with you.

This simple exercise will shift your life and gratify you in a way you might not have experienced before.

For years, I have been working to find gratitude for each and every moment of my life. But when I began reporting those small moments for which I was grateful, I noticed a surprising result: I felt more joyful.

The more gratitude I discovered and shared, the more elation I felt—and the longer it lasted. Gratitude is the foundation for joy, and who doesn't want more joy in their lives? I call the person with whom I share my Bliss Buddy.

This book is all about finding and sharing with your own Bliss Buddy- someone who'll help make your happiness greater.

In the following pages you'll learn the power of connecting with someone for the sole purpose of sharing your daily wonder and bliss. You will also learn why finding and sharing blissful moments can be so life-changing.

Since I started matching Bliss Buddy pairs in 2014, I have heard from many people that they are more open to moments of appreciation and delight in their lives. I am convinced that having a Bliss Buddy can be one of the most meaningful practices you can undertake to find a happier life.

Throughout this book, on the left-hand pages, you'll see quotes from Bliss Buddies that describe the experiences they have had.

In other words, don't just "take it from me."

"I jump out of bed in the morning and can't wait to read and write my Bliss Buddy email. I have a relationship with my Buddy like no other in my life.

She is there for me, cheering me on, when things are good and she helps me to get through the Bliss-less days.

It is awesome to walk this journey of softer, kinder, happier with her."

Angela Piatelli, Naples, FL

Why Have a Buddy?

Things are just more rewarding when you do them with friends. I often start something new, like a diet or exercise plan, with a buddy.

I know there will be someone in the trenches with me, cheering me on, celebrating my success and someone to lean on when the going gets tough.

This is the essence of the project: Finding a Bliss Buddy to share your gratitude with. Gratitude grows exponentially when you share it with someone—especially with someone who is invested in celebrating your gratitude.

"I do feel like it has made me aware of trying to find at least one good thing in a day—especially if it's a crappy day!

I also feel like I have been more conscious of trying to hold on to a moment or happy feeling and really turn it into a memory—really experience that moment/feeling entirely."

Nell Reid, Maplewood, NJ

In life, there is no escaping hardship. We all experience sadness, illness and eventually, the death of a loved one. We need some tools to help find the silver lining in the midst of all that.

When you live with gratitude, and you notice those tiny bursts of happiness that pop up all around you, you find the key to living a life filled with joy. That's why having someone to be accountable to, and who will be accountable to you, is essential for making sure you take time every day to be grateful.

This practice helps you get through the difficult days more easily.

I often teach my students that when your toilet overflows try to focus on how grateful you are to have a toilet!

"So many people say, 'It's the little things.' YES it is. This is not about searching for the grand gestures or the monumental moments. Those don't happen all that often.

Instead, it is about taking it down to the smallest moments and as you do, stringing those together to build a life that is joyful. It's not always easy, especially when things get tough."

Andi Hessekiel, Rye, NY

It's the Little Things

Having a Bliss Buddy turns you into a detective for your own happiness. It encourages you to be on the lookout for all the small, yet blissful moments that arise throughout your day.

Sometimes it's just that Starbucks got your name right, or that the perfect parking space opened up as you arrived on the street. When you train your attention to "Notice" these joyful moments, you begin to realize that there are so many of them right before your eyes.

"When we were communicating every day, there were times when I felt I had no bliss to report, but then, I learned to focus on smaller things that I wouldn't have pinpointed or noticed as a blissful moment to be grateful for.

It was more than just noticing them and moving on. I was able to pinpoint what about these certain things made me happy and, even if I was having a mundane day, I would focus on what I am thankful for in my life on a micro level."

Sophie Lavin, New York, NY

One of the many places I teach meditation and mindfulness is at Campowerment (*www.Campowerment.com*), a sleepaway camp-inspired long-weekend retreat for grown-up women, which incorporates play and the freedom of summer camp with the adult lessons of living your best life.

It was at Campowerment in March of 2014 that I started pairing "Bliss Buddies," and the Bliss Buddy Project was born. The idea was to pair people together who would commit to sharing bliss moments, via email or text, for 30 days. "All you'd need to do," I told the campers, "is to notice one blissful moment in your day—something that you feel grateful for—write it down and send it off to your Buddy."

It could be as simple as this: "Today when I walked outside the sun shone on my face."

"Whatever happens, only good comes from taking note of those small, blissful moments. It brightens your day and cultivates strength to take you through the inevitable challenging times. My Bliss Buddy is now a treasured friend with whom I trust my bliss but also the sad times. The consistent, loving support has been a true blessing in my life."

Jana Schey, Houston, TX

The Power of Two

I paired up with Jana and we have communicated since the very beginning. Never did I imagine that we would still be in contact all these years later! An added bonus of our Bliss Buddy pairing is the deep friendship that developed, one of the most special I have in my life.

I have since connected 100 pairs of Buddies, who have been communicating their bliss with each other from across the country. I hear from them regularly, and they all report that their frequent check-ins have made a huge difference in their lives.

"Knowing Stacey is there and that she is so awesome helps me to feel supported and seen.

As an online persona, it's sometimes feels like I become a product.

When I have wins, she is genuinely happy for me and supports me to keep going."

Beth Nydick, Livingston, NJ

For most people, staying on top of any daily practice such as exercise, meditation or gratitude, can be a challenge. Let's face it, we all have such busy lives, and we often don't put ourselves at the top of our to-do lists. I ask new Bliss Buddies to commit to a 30-day practice. Then, if they chose to continue, communication may become more intermittent.

One of the beautiful things about my relationship with Jana is knowing that we are just an email or text or Facebook message away from each other. No matter how long we go between touching base, we can always pick right back up.

When you're sharing a beautiful moment, it's as if no time at all has gone by.

When lovely things happen during the day I am often inspired to think about Jana. I try right in that moment to stop and share with her. Modern technology allows us instant communication with nearly everyone, so why not take advantage of it?

Writing down the bliss moment solidifies it for me, and even if I don't hear back, I've paused to take note of that day's small instant in time that I am thankful for, and in doing so, sealed it in my brain and created a memory.

This practice is a two-way street. It is as much a benefit for the recipient as it is for the sender. I get excited every time I hear from Jana! When I receive a text or email from her it always lifts my spirits. She also does something no one else in my life does that I love … she mails me postcards from far away destinations when she travels the world for work and play. Old fashion mail is a lost art and I am always so thankful to receive a card with beautiful scenery and a sweet message from her.

"It's made me slow down a bit. When I have a bliss moment and write it down, it makes me pause a little longer, enjoy the bliss a minute more and realize that happiness doesn't have to be this huge 'Oh-my-God-I-can't-believe-this-happened' moment."

Cari Gelber, New York, NY

How can an email or text change your life? By itself, it probably won't. But a series of them can. Change won't happen immediately, especially because life has a way of roaring back at you between Bliss Buddy communiqués. Trying to hold onto the good can be super challenging. Gradually, with consistency, you will begin to view life from a more positive perspective which in turn will make you feel optimistic.

Remember, this is a practice. Just like daily meditation, it is never a mastery.

As the late, great artist Prince said, "We are all just trying to get through this thing called LIFE."

"Noticing and recording my bliss is bringing me more self-knowledge, which allows me to make choices that increase my bliss! Pretty cool!"

Sara Alyea, Hopewell, NJ

Practicing Gratitude With
a Bliss Buddy Will Change You

People who've been doing this for a while notice that their attitude toward life begins to shift in slight or dramatic ways.

Take Sara. In her search to find things to share with her Buddy Sonya, she noticed that her bliss communication was often about how happy she was when she bought fresh flowers. Sara then decided to spend a little more time at the market each week, really looking at and enjoying the flowers she found there.

Sure, it took a little longer to go to the market each time, but the extra 10 minutes increased her bliss. She had made a conscious decision to change her habits, based on what she noticed about her messages to her Bliss Buddy.

Having a Bliss Buddy gives you permission—in fact encourages you—to register bliss in the tiniest ways and relish the moment.

Think about it—if you mentioned to someone that you saw a cloud in the shape of a heart and that made you glad, they might think you were a little daft. But your Bliss Buddy is primed for your observation and will probably congratulate you on this discovery.

Good NEWS About
The Bliss Buddy Project

Now that you understand how having a Bliss Buddy makes finding gratitude all the more satisfying, you may be wondering how you can get started.

I created the "Good NEWS" system for helping Bliss Buddies find their bliss. It's an acronym that can guide you to uncovering what makes you feel light-hearted and thankful; then how to make the most of it. NEWS stands for:

*N*otice your small moment

*E*xperience it

Write it down

Share it

"I'm always on the hunt for bliss moments and things to be grateful for that I can share and explore on my own and with Ellen!"

Nadine Kerstan, Short Hills, NJ

N = Notice

NOTICE a small moment that makes you smile. This is the first step to cultivating a practice of gratitude. Make a choice every day to look for pleasing or beautiful things you might ordinarily overlook. Once you begin turning your attention to these small occurrences, you will NOTICE them almost everywhere. It's incredible how quickly they show up when you go looking for them.

"Naming, feeling and expressing gratitude brings me joy in the moment.

Moments build and extend into periods of time, periods of time expand into days. Shifts are occurring.

I feel more joy, peace and calm. I feel held and protected, guided and inspired."

Tara Prupis, Millburn, NJ

E = Experience

EXPERIENCE through all your senses, your moment of joy. First, stop and take a breath. Then ask yourself: What am I seeing? What am I feeling? What am I hearing, tasting and smelling right now? I don't know about you, but often when I order a cup of coffee at Starbucks, my name is wrong!

So, let's say your bliss moment is when Starbucks finally gets your name right. Stop where you are—see your name on the cup. Smell the coffee around you. Listen to the sounds of the barista making lattes. Feel the warmth of the cup in your hand. Take a sip. Taste that delicious brew which has your correct name on the cup. With all of your senses working together, you can turn this simple moment into a strong and gratifying memory.

Being fully present allows us to wring the most pleasure out of life. How do you know when you're present? You are not thinking about the past or the future. Instead, you are fully right where you are. It is possible to live in the moment, but to do so, you need to focus your attention and notice all that is happening around you.

W = Write it down

WRITE down your joyful moment on paper, on a Post-It, in an email or text. Research [2] suggests that writing things down helps you remember them because it causes the brain to store the information more efficiently. As you write down your bliss, you create a visual memory that solidifies and internalizes what you observed. Writing makes it more real. Joy accumulates, so try to remember the happy snippets you encounter all day long. As you tally them you will begin to sense a soft, subtle contentment that settles over you.

"I do my very best to stop each day—or as often as possible—to take notice of the things, big and small, that bring bliss into my life. I notice things that I may have missed previously. Also, I am so grateful to have such a close-knit and trusted relationship with a wonderful Bliss Buddy. We allow the other person to know us on a much more personal basis. We can open up. We can share without fear of being judged. Through our emails we laugh together, we cry together, and we always send love and virtual hugs."

Phyllis Shinbane, Calabasas, CA

S = Share

SHARE your little bursts of satisfaction with someone. Taking the time to share your joy helps it amplify. Joy gets paid forward just by declaring your excitement over the smallest of things, it's that simple! By committing to do this regularly, you become accountable to your Bliss Buddy, and you will continue to notice those moments. And this becomes a circular exercise because when you have to share something from your day, you begin to NOTICE. Now you are on the lookout for those bright moments and that makes you more present because you are paying attention.

When you're paying attention, you can fully take in all that is around you. That's when you will begin to experience those "aha" moments that can truly shift your life.

"I don't 'gloss over' or dismiss the small things that make me happy. No matter how nerdy they are. If it makes me bliss out, it's really cool!"

Karen Elder, Los Angeles, CA

The More You Share, the More Grateful You Become

As you can see, the Bliss Buddy Project was a good idea that has turned into a powerful force for developing gratitude. It's simple and it's effective. All it takes is to make a commitment to do this with someone and share an email or a text for 30 consecutive days. Here's an email I recently sent, with the subject line "Bliss": "I found a feather on my walk this morning!"

And a recent text I sent showed a picture of a front yard with the following message: "Fresh snow. My bliss today. So beautiful."

"It is good to get someone else's perspective about what is bliss, someone who lives a completely different life than me, and whose path, under different circumstances, I would not cross."

Joanna Kleinman, Cherry Hill, NJ

Make the Commitment

Do it for a month, just to get yourself in the habit. After that, you and your Bliss Buddy may decide to check in less frequently. However, you will have begun a life-shifting process of searching for little things to be thankful for. Once you begin to find those small moments of delight, you will also discover that your life is happier, more hopeful and more full of positivity. You will begin to appreciate what you have and focus less on what you lack. That's a lot of bang for your "Good NEWS" buck.

Find Your Bliss Buddy

You can find your own Bliss Buddy. Ask a friend, a neighbor, a co-worker, your cousin, or even your sibling. Ask your friend at the gym or that person you see each week when you drop your child at ballet or baseball. It doesn't have to be someone you know well. It only needs to be someone who is willing to share and wants to feel a little merrier every day.

Some of the most enduring Bliss Buddy relationships have grown between people who barely knew each other at the start, like Jana and me. Maybe that's the strength of those partnerships—each person is able to appreciate the other's joy without attaching any judgment. What I have found is that friendships often develop through the sharing.

However, you could do this successfully with someone you know, someone who is close to you. All it takes is an understanding that you will both be looking for ways to uncover bliss in your lives.

"I really enjoy having a Bliss Buddy. It's nice to be able to talk to someone who lives half-way across the country, who barely knows me, but who is also a person that wants to find more bliss in her life! I love it and find more happiness in each day!"

Eliana Goldman, New York, NY

I hope now you want to run out and find yourself a Bliss Buddy! If you are searching and are unable to connect with someone, please visit my website where I can help with a Bliss Buddy:

mindfulnessmeetingplace.com/ blissbuddyproject

Here are some ideas that may help you find your Bliss! I hope these short prompts begin to guide you on your journey.

Today notice something in nature.

Today notice something you have accomplished.

Today notice something that someone in your family or your pet does.

Today notice something kind you did for someone else.

Today notice something that someone created.

Today notice something you hear.

Today notice something you feel.

Today notice something you see.

Today notice something you smell.

Today notice something you taste.

One Final Thought

The week before I sent this finished manuscript to print, I got a flat tire on my way to work. It was pouring rain and the tow company said it would take at least an hour-and-a-half before they could get to me. This meant I had to not only miss the three classes I was scheduled to teach that morning, but that I'd be sitting in the car alone, feeling frustrated, impatient, disappointed and stressed! After calling work, figuring out logistics, and meditating for 15 minutes, I texted Jana, my Bliss Buddy.

"So right now, I am sitting waiting for a tow truck," I wrote. "I hit a pothole in the rain and instantly got a flat tire. Taking a few deep breaths, I realized I am grateful to have a wonderful book on Audible that I can listen to as I sit and wait. I am making this my Bliss moment!" Jana's response was the best reinforcement: "And this is a perfect example of resilience. Good luck with the tire."

Having a Bliss Buddy practice has changed the way I walk through the world. In that flat tire moment, I looked for something I could share with Jana and I found it. Reaching out to her helped transform that challenging situation into one of calm and, frankly, enjoyment as I listened to my book and steered clear of negativity. It is now a way of life to choose gratitude over almost anything else when faced with tough times. All it takes is a little dedication and discipline, and the recognition that it's always a good time to be grateful.

References

[1] Emmons, Robert. *Thanks! How Practicing Gratitude Can Make You Happier*. Mariner Books (reprint edition), 2008.

[2] Dr. Karin Harman James and Atwood, T.P. "The role of sensori-motor learning in the perception of letter-like forms: tracking the causes of neural specialization for letters." *Cognitive Neuropsychology*, February 2009.

Acknowledgements

Thank you, thank you, THANK YOU to my dear friend and consummate editor Andrea Atkins Hessekiel. You have known me since childhood and I can't imagine my life without you in it. You know my history and my heart, you are a shoulder to cry on and someone who makes me laugh at myself and life in the best way. My life is richer for having you in it. I love you.

To Judy Malamed, for your dedication to proofing this manuscript and for your deep and abiding friendship. I love you, Lucy. Yours always, Ethel.

To Beth Sandweiss, from the moment I first sat in your meditation class, you changed my life. You are my teacher, my mentor, my friend. I love you.

To Sarah McLean, thank you from the bottom of my heart. Thank you for guiding me on this teacher path. My training as a meditation and mindfulness instructor, through The McLean Meditation Institute, has been invaluable. I now know my purpose is to make the world more peaceful one person at a time, and in aligning with that purpose, I find deep contentment. I am forever grateful to be a part of the MMI teacher sangha. I love being in your radiant light and I love you.

To Juliet Dombrowski from Julietrose.info for my beautiful author photo.

To Sean Hoade, my book formatter, for making this daunting process so easy.

And to my husband, my Barton, my greatest cheerleader. When I embarked on this path of meditation, I always felt your love and support lifting me up. You have brought me endless bliss moments since we first met, moments each day when we laugh together. I am blessed to have found you, my love, my Soulmate. I will remain always and forever your Channie.

And, of course, to all the Bliss Buddy pairs out there, thank you for making my dream come alive and for elevating the force field of joy in the world.

About the Author

Anne Sussman is the creator of The Bliss Buddy Project, which grew out of her work as a Meditation and Mindfulness Instructor. As the founder of Mindfulness Meeting Place, Anne helps individuals live better by teaching the benefits and practice of meditation and mindfulness. She received her certification as a Mindfulness and Meditation Instructor, and a MMI-Mindfulness@Work Trainer at the McLean Meditation Institute.

Anne teaches meditation to individuals and groups and also offers mindfulness training to businesses around the country. She is the resident meditation teacher at Campowerment, a retreat that helps people reconnect with their purpose through a fun-filled camp experience. Anne is not a guru, or a spiritual healer, but someone just like you, struggling to live in our fast-paced, often stress-filled world, who has seen the remarkable benefits that meditating consistently brings.

Anne is passionate about helping to heal the world of food insecurity. A portion of the proceeds of this book will be donated to the Interfaith Food Pantry of the Oranges in Orange, New Jersey. Anne is the mother of two amazing grown sons, Josh and Max, and her fabulous daughter-in-love, Erin. She lives in Maplewood, N.J. with her husband.

If the only prayer you ever say in your life is "Thank you," it will be enough.

Meister Eckhart